First Facts™

Health Matters

Pinkeye

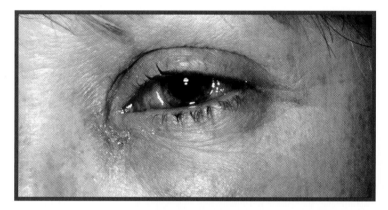

by Jason Glaser

Consultant:
James R. Hubbard, MD
Fellow in the American Academy of Pediatrics
Iowa Medical Society
West Des Moines, Iowa

Capstone *press*

Mankato, Minnesota

First Facts is published by Capstone Press,
151 Good Counsel Drive, P.O. Box 669, Mankato, Minnesota 56002.
www.capstonepress.com

Library of Congress Cataloging-in-Publication Data
Glaser, Jason.
    Pinkeye / by Jason Glaser.
    p. cm.—(First facts. Health matters)
    Summary: "Introduces pinkeye, its causes, symptoms, treatments, and prevention"
—Provided by publisher.
    Includes bibliographical references and index.
    ISBN 0-7368-4292-6 (hardcover)
    1. Conjunctivitis—Juvenile literature. I. Title. II. Series.
RE320.G56 2006
617.7'73—dc22   2004031054

Editorial Credits
Mari C. Schuh, editor; Juliette Peters, designer; Kelly Garvin, photo researcher/photo editor

Photo Credits
Capstone Press/Karon Dubke, cover (foreground), 9, 14, 15, 19, 21
Corbis/Rosa & Rosa, 8
NASA Johnson Space Center, 20
Photo Researchers Inc./Dr. Chris Hale, 11; Dr. P. Marazzi, 1, 6–7, 16–17; SPL, 5 (inset);
    University, "La Sapienza," Rome/Dept. of Anatomy/Prof. P. Motta, cover (background);
    VEM, 5
Superstock Inc., 12–13

Table of Contents

What Is Pinkeye?

Pinkeye is an eye illness. Pinkeye is caused by tiny germs called **viruses** and **bacteria**. Germs can get into the eye and make it hurt. Parts inside the eye swell up. Then the white part of the eye turns pink or red.

 Fact!
Tears help clear particles out of the eye. Babies can get pinkeye if their tear ducts are shut.

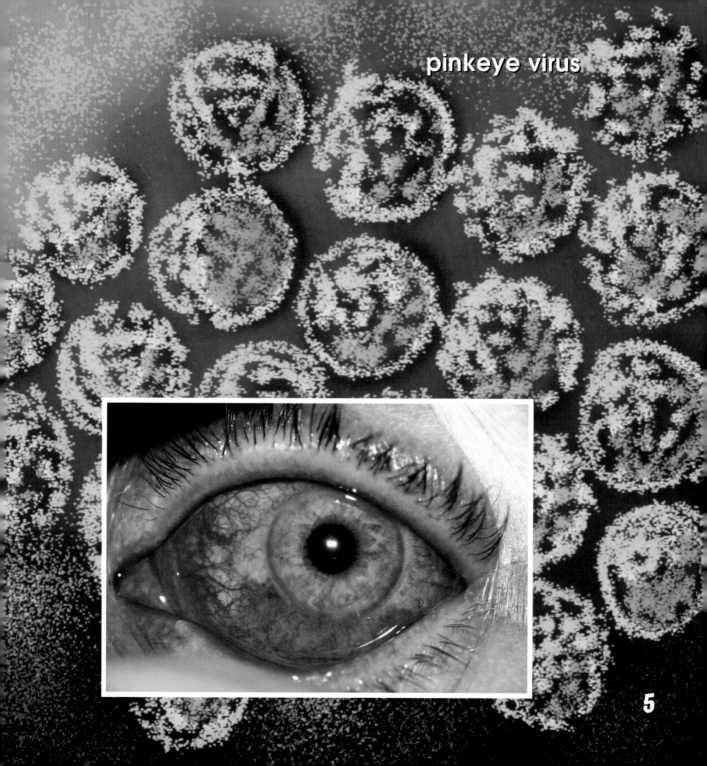

pinkeye virus

5

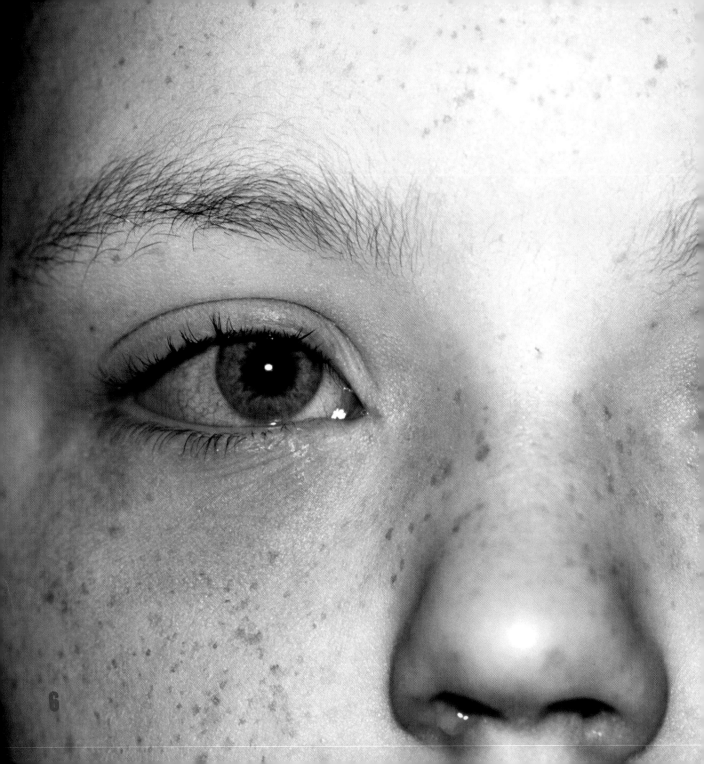

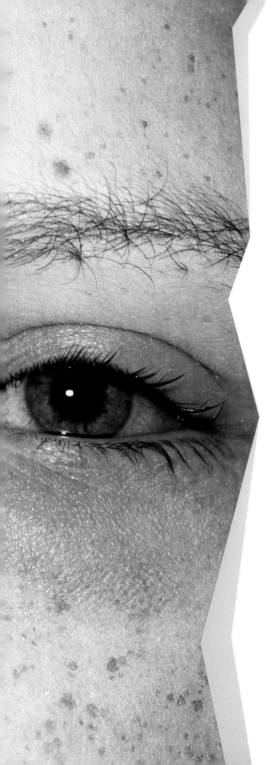

Signs of Pinkeye

Pink or red eyes are the main signs of pinkeye. The eyelids may also turn red.

Pinkeye makes the eyes itch and hurt. The eyes may make tears or a sticky fluid. This fluid can cause eyelashes to stick shut.

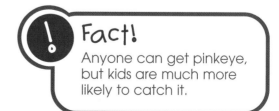

Fact!
Anyone can get pinkeye, but kids are much more likely to catch it.

How Do Kids Get Pinkeye?

Kids often get pinkeye from other kids. Kids with pinkeye get germs on their hands and towels. Other kids touch the germs, then touch their eyes.

Many kids get pinkeye from
allergies. Dust and smoke can
hurt the eyes and cause pinkeye.

What Else Could It Be?

Not all eye problems are pinkeye. Eyes can turn red from being injured, scratched, or hit. The eye will usually be red around the scratch.

Some people get an eye illness called iritis. The colored part of their eye is hurt. The eye is red and may be painful.

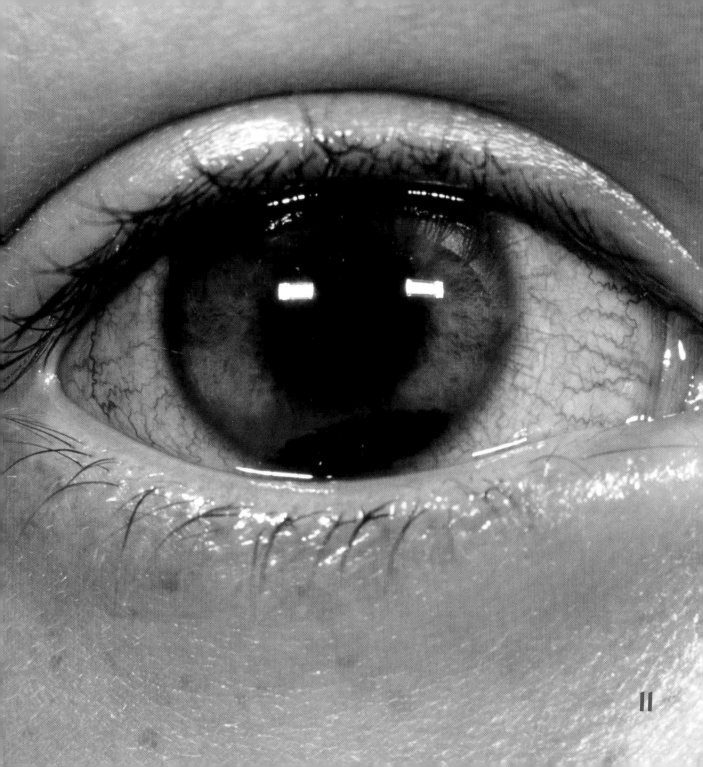

Should Kids See a Doctor?

Kids should see a doctor for pinkeye. The doctor can test for germs in the eye. Kids might need **medicine** or eyedrops. Kids with pinkeye may have to stay home from school. Then others won't catch pinkeye.

Fact!
Some kinds of pinkeye go away in two to three days. Other kinds last two to three weeks.

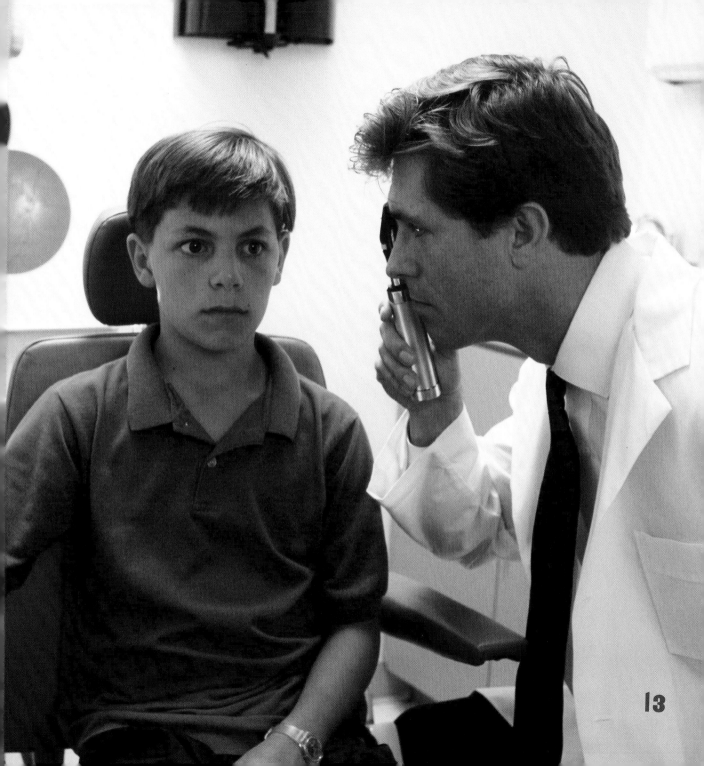

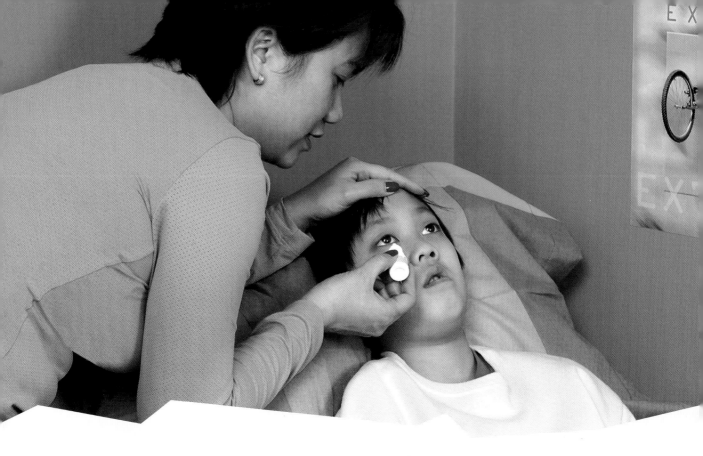

How to Treat Pinkeye

Most often, people use eyedrops to treat pinkeye. Eyedrops stop itching and help get rid of pinkeye. A warm, wet washcloth can get rid of sticky fluids.

People with pinkeye should wash their hands often. They can use tissues to wipe their eyes. They should not share towels with others.

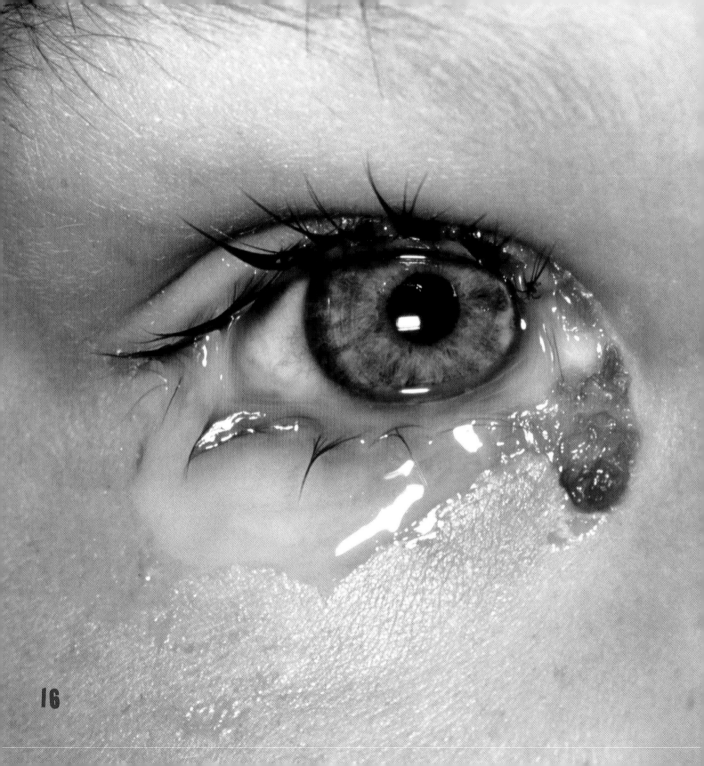

If It Gets Worse

If pinkeye gets worse, the eyes can be damaged. Kids should see a doctor again if their pinkeye is not getting better.

Pinkeye germs can spread to other parts of the body. The germs can get into the throat or ears. A person can get a sore throat or an earache.

Staying Healthy

Clean hands can help people avoid pinkeye. People should wash their hands often. Hands should be cleaned before touching the face or eyes. To keep hands clean, use a tissue to touch your face or eyes. Then germs won't get on your hands.

Fact!

In 2002, 500 students at Dartmouth College got pinkeye. Some people think the students got it by touching computer keyboards.

Amazing but True!

In many countries, pinkeye is known as Apollo disease. In 1969, the country Ghana had many cases of pinkeye. These cases happened around the same time as the Apollo 11 moon landing. Some people thought the pinkeye was a curse caused by the moon landing.

Hands On: Protective Tears

Pinkeye can cause lots of tears. Your body uses tears to protect your eyes. Ask an adult to help you with this activity.

What You Need

fresh onion   small container
adult   wet washcloth
kitchen knife

What You Do

1. Peel off the outer layer of the onion.
2. Have an adult cut the onion into small pieces.
3. Put the onion pieces into the container.
4. Sniff into the container. The cut onions will make your eyes water.
5. Gently wipe your eyes with the wet washcloth.

The onion gives off a gas when it is chopped. The gas mixes with water in your eyes to make an acid. Your eyes make tears to wash away the acid. When you get pinkeye, your body makes tears to wash out the pinkeye virus.

Glossary

allergies (AL-er-jeez)—reactions to things like dogs, cats, and dust; allergies cause runny noses, sneezing, and watery eyes.

bacteria (bak-TEER-ee-uh)—very tiny living creatures

medicine (MED-uh-suhn)—pills or syrup that can make people feel better during an illness

virus (VYE-ruhss)—a germ that copies itself inside the body's cells

Read More

Gordon, Sharon. *Pinkeye.* Rookie Read-About Health. New York: Children's Press, 2003.

Rice, Judith. *Those Ooey Gooey Winky-Blinky But—Invisible Pinkeye Germs.* St. Paul, Minn.: Redleaf Press, 2000.

Royston, Angela. *Pink Eye.* It's Catching. Chicago: Heinemann, 2002.

Internet Sites

FactHound offers a safe, fun way to find Internet sites related to this book. All of the sites on FactHound have been researched by our staff.

Here's how:
1. Visit *www.facthound.com*
2. Type in this special code **0736842926** for age-appropriate sites. Or enter a search word related to this book for a more general search.
3. Click on the **Fetch It** button.

FactHound will fetch the best sites for you!

Index